FIGHT
THE GOOD FIGHT

Unveiling The Secretes Of Spiritual Warfare And How To Remain Victorious

By: Apostle L'Tanya C. Perry, MDiv.

Paperback ISBN: 978-1-957052-87-8

Hardcover- ISBN: 978-1-957052-90-8

Printed in the United States of America.

TAP📖Press

TAP Press Publishing: Contact us at hello@ltanyaperry.com

Dedication

I want to thank my Mom for working with me hand in hand in prayer services when deliverance would pop off. You were right there interceding for me and others while warring in the spirit, declaring God's Word over satanic powers. Healing would take place when men and women are free from demonic oppression. I remember nights when witches and warlocks tried to attack us. I never forget the high level of attacks. Nights when my children couldn't sleep and all kinds of evil were sent to us throughout the night. My kitchen floor and outside living area would be the deliverance area. Thank you, Mom, for helping me pray for my family.

I learned so much on the battlefield. As my little niece Maya said to me, "Auntie, God always wins." That's so true! God always wins. To my husband, thank you for being open to God to grow us in the warfare. We never gave up despite the fight.

To my children Alexus and KJ, you guys didn't grow up on coloring books and Bible stories. You knew and experienced God's presence and how powerful God destroys the works of the devil at a very young age. Don't let the devil rule your life because you are in your flesh. Discipline yourselves and let God be God no matter what the situation.

To all New Beginnings Worship Center Citizens, you have grown so much, so keep the faith and keep being open and welcoming the move of God in your lives. And to you, yes you, holding this book, this warfare book is the first in the warfare prayer series. However, I encourage you to read the entire prayer book series. This book is the foundation of warfare; we have an assurance that we are more than conquerors (Romans 8:37). So, keep victory in sight, and we shall win.

Table of Contents

INTRODUCTION

There are many teachings in the body of Christ concerning spiritual warfare, most of them extreme and unscriptural. But now, more than ever, what believers need is not a plethora of teachings, but accurate and life-applicable ones based on the Word of God. Wrong teachings lead to wrong beliefs and wrong Christian practices that make us unfruitful as believers.

Also, complex teachings on Christian subjects such as spiritual warfare confuse and deter people. They become indifferent and passive concerning vital kingdom truths. The Bible in John chapter 1 talks about the Word—Jesus—as the true light that shines in darkness and prevails over it. That's the kind of Word or teaching that produces a life of victory.

One major ingredient that determines victory in spiritual warfare is accurate knowledge, that's why I wrote this book. Even in natural warfare, military intelligence is vital and determines victory or defeat. Therefore, you can't fight and win if you're ignorant. Warfare and ignorance are incompatible; you must know your enemy.

Many believers don't even know there's a warfare. Some are aware but indifferent, not knowing that they have a role to play. Others are aware and involved but don't know why there's a warfare and how to fight successfully. No matter what category you fall under, the problem is a certain degree of ignorance.

It's All About Faith

There is a spiritual warfare because there's a spiritual enemy. The Bible reveals that believers have an enemy and he is "looking for whom to devour", trying to "get an advantage" over you, seeking to get a "foothold" in your life and is "accusing" you before God.

The good news is, the Bible also reveals that our victory over the enemy is not just a possibility, but a reality. Jesus' death, burial and resurrection is the basis of our victory. He conquered sin, the grave and satan for our sake. As a result, everyone born of God overcomes. This shows that there will be contention and opposition— hence, the need to overcome—but at the end, we've been fully equipped to triumph.

However, there's a silent question that needs to be answered. If our victory over the enemy is guaranteed in Christ, why is there a warfare? It's because of the object of contention. The enemy is after your faith because the moment you lose your faith, you've lost the battle.

The enemy is out to ensure you don't believe you're saved, healed, forgiven, protected, restored and more. His aim is to challenge everything God says you are, because he can't harm you until you stop believing God. God says you're more than a conqueror, but the enemy says you're defeated.

It's faith in Christ's sacrifice that makes you a believer, and it's in faith in the victory produced by that sacrifice that makes you more than a conqueror. The believer who doesn't know this will rollover or throw in the towel when assaulted by the enemy.

Spiritual warfare has to do with maintaining your Christian faith and resisting everything that wants to distract and hinder you from fulfilling your divine calling. The word "calling" in Christianity is often associated with ministry. However, it isn't only relevant to those chosen by God to be apostles, evangelists, prophets, pastors and teachers. The word "calling" in Scripture also means divine election into faith in Christ Jesus.

War A Good Warfare

In Acts 2, when Peter witnessed to the multitude about the resurrection of Christ, the promise of the Holy Spirit and the way to salvation, he said in verse 39, *"For the promise is unto you, and to your children, and to all that are afar off, even as many as the Lord our God shall call."* The Amplified Bible says, *"as many as the Lord our God invites and bids to come to Himself."* So you see that there's a general call of salvation that refers to every aspect of our walk with God. In truth, no man can walk with God except he is called to do so. (Genesis 17:1)

Ephesians 1:18 talks about *"the hope of our calling,"* also referring to the life of faith. Paul was saying that there's a reason God saved us from a life of sin to walk with Him, and his prayer for the Church was that they would come to understand it.

While spiritual warfare includes encountering and prevailing over satan and his forces, that's not all spiritual warfare is about. Kenneth E. Hagin said, "Genuine spiritual warfare has to do mostly with the mind and the flesh and fighting the good fight of faith." [1]

When Paul mentioned "war" and "warfare" in his epistle to Timothy, his son in the Lord, it was about fulfilling his ministry in the light of the prophecies he'd received about himself. He said, *"This charge I commit unto thee, son Timothy, according to the prophecies which went before on thee, that thou by them mightiest war a good warfare."* (1 Timothy 1:18 [KJV]) That is to say, Timothy was to maintain his faith and fulfil "the hope of his calling."

Likewise, to be successful in your walk with God and accomplish all that God created you to do on earth, you must war a good warfare. Spiritual warfare exists because there are many opposing forces trying to stop you from pressing toward the mark of your high calling in Christ Jesus (as Paul puts it).

FIGHT THE GOOD FIGHT is a handbook on spiritual warfare with all the spiritual artillery you need to fight the good fight of faith. It's message—which comes from years of experience on the field, studying the Scriptures and divine revelation—is Scriptural, practical and balanced. Within its pages, age-long Bible truths are communicated simply but with the power of the Holy Spirit.

Learn about the weapons of our warfare, how to discern the enemy's devices, how to be a good soldier and many other powerful kingdom secrets that will make you an overcomer in your daily life.

Chapter 1

HOW IT ALL STARTED

Everything that we see has a beginning. Life wasn't always chaotic. There was a point when all things were peaceful and in order. There was a point when there was no need to worry about a possible evil planned against you. But how did it all started?

The term spiritual warfare describes an unending battle between the church and the devil with his angels.[2] Yes, the statement isn't clearly written in the Scriptures but it derived from various descriptions of the everyday struggles of the Christian life. Apostle Paul writes (Ephesians 6:10-13 [ESV]), *"Finally, be strong in the Lord and in the strength of His might. Put on the whole armor of God, that you may be able to stand against the schemes of the devil. For we do not wrestle against flesh and blood, but against the rulers, against the authorities, against the cosmic powers over this present darkness, against the spiritual forces of evil in the heavenly places. Therefore, take up the whole armor of God, that you may be able to withstand in the evil day, and having done all, to stand firm."*

The verses above looks like a war posture. It's a call to all believers to maintain a battle ready position. But how did we get here? Let's cycle back to the very beginning. All through the Scriptures we see different description of how beautiful heaven is. It a peaceful place. A place of joy and harmony. Where God sits on the throne surrounded by the twenty four elders, worshipping Him. It's a place of manifestation of God's glory.

Here is a brief description in (Revelations 21:18-23 [ERV]), *"The wall was made of jasper. The city was made of pure gold, as pure as glass. The foundation stones of the city walls had every kind of expensive jewels in them. The first foundation stone was jasper, the second was sapphire, the third was chalcedony, the fourth was emerald, the fifth was onyx, the sixth was carnelian, the seventh was yellow quartz, the eighth was beryl, the ninth was topaz, the tenth was chrysoprase, the eleventh was jacinth, and the twelfth was amethyst. The twelve gates were twelve pearls. Each gate was made from one pearl. The street of the city was made of pure gold, as clear as glass. I did not see a temple in the city. The Lord God All-Powerful and the Lamb were the city's temple. The city did not need the sun or the moon to shine on it. The glory of God gave the city light. The Lamb was the city's lamp."*

I saw a poem that describes the beauty of heaven that will make anyone want to go there right away. It writes;

"I'm going where the rainbows glow
And the clouds will never cry.
The sun will sit upon the Earth
To warm the heavens with its shine.

Where the sweetest scent of the roses
Will be carried with the breeze
To mingle with the garden fruits.
The butterflies and the bees,
The birds will sing together,
And the nights will all be day.
The stars will forever twinkle
And the flowers will never fade.
So this is where you will find me
When my time on Earth is done.
I'll go to be in this great heaven
With all of God's chosen ones."[3]

In addition to the structural beauty of heaven. God also had one of His cherub names Lucifer. The Book of Ezekiel, (Ezekiel 28:11-14 [ESV]) describes him a bit, *"Moreover, the Word of the LORD came to me: "Son of man, raise a lamentation over the king of Tyre, and say to him, Thus says the Lord GOD: "You were the signet of perfection, full of wisdom and perfect in beauty. You were in Eden, the garden of God; every precious stone was your covering, sardius, topaz, and diamond, beryl, onyx, and jasper, sapphire, emerald, and carbuncle; and crafted in gold were your settings and your engravings. On the day that you were created they were prepared. You were an anointed guardian cherub. I placed you; you were on the holy mountain of God; in the midst of the stones of fire you walked."*

He was part of God's perfect work until he became rebellious. (Ezekiel 28:15-16 [ESV]) says, *"You were blameless in your ways from the day you were created, till unrighteousness was found in you. In the abundance of your trade you were filled with violence in your midst, and you sinned; so I cast you as a profane thing from the mountain of God, and I destroyed you, O guardian cherub, from the midst of the stones of fire."*

This perfect work of God suddenly rose against God. The Bible says in (Isaiah 14:11-15 [ERV]), *"Your pride has been sent down to Sheol. The music from your harps announces the coming of your proud spirit. Maggots will be the bed you lie on, and other worms will cover your body like a blanket. You were like the morning star, but you have fallen from the sky. In the past, all the nations on earth bowed down before you, but now you have been cut down. You always told yourself, "I will go to the skies above. I will put my throne above God's stars. I will sit on Zaphon, the holy mountain where the gods meet. I will go up to the altar above the tops of the clouds. I will be like God Most High." But that did not happen. You were brought down to the deep pit—Sheol, the place of death."*

He lifted up himself in pride and wanted to be like God. He felt he was perfect enough for his position in the spectrum of heavens operation. He felt he needed more. He wanted more authority and more dominion. He wanted to reign more. He admired the One on heaven's throne and wished it could be himself. He admired how everyone bowed to the Lordship of the Father and it feels good to be the one. His strongest desire was to be like God. So how did he go about executing this thought?

The Bible says in (Revelations 12:7-9 [NKJV]), *"And war broke out in heaven: Michael and his angels fought with the dragon; and the dragon and his angels fought, but they did not prevail, nor was a place found for them in heaven any longer. So, the great dragon was cast out, that serpent of old, called the devil and satan, who deceives the whole world; he was cast to the earth, and his angels were cast out with him."* satan's strategy to execute his plan was to start up war in heaven. He instigated one-third of the angels to support his agenda and they planned out war in heaven. The place of peace and harmony was suddenly throne into chaos because one angel wanted to be more than who he was.

This was how it all started. Spiritual warfare didn't start from you, it started right in heaven. Spiritual warfare existed long before God created man. This war birthed two kingdoms- the kingdom of God and the kingdom of satan. The good news is that satan lost the battle in heaven. Michael and his angels fought and prevailed. At the end satan was cast to the earth. His migration to the earth was the beginning of warfare on the earth. He wanted to rise above God and now he is even below men. One can envision the intensity of the anger he brought upon his arrival to the earth.

The Scripture says in (Revelations 12:10-12 [NET]), *"Then I heard a loud voice in heaven saying, "The salvation and the power and the kingdom of our God, and the ruling authority of his Christ, have now come, because the accuser of our brothers and sisters, the one who accuses them day and night before our God, has been thrown down. But they overcame him by the blood of the Lamb and by the word of their testimony, and they did not love their lives so much that they were afraid to die. Therefore, your heavens rejoice, and all who reside in them! But woe to the earth and the sea because the devil has come down to you! He is filled with terrible anger, for he knows that he only has a little time!"*

Did you see that? Heaven fought against satan and won, so the battle ground was moved to the earth. The door of heaven was shut permanently against satan and his fallen angels. He has no place in heaven anymore neither can he stir up war in heaven. But the Bible says, "Woe to the inhabitants of the earth." The devil came to the earth with that wrath to continue the battle on the earth. The once peaceful earth that God created and saw that it was good, now plays host to angry satan. This is how it all started.

It didn't start with you neither would it end with you. The battle was moved from heaven to the earth and we are all part of it. So, when you see people contending with you or planning your downfall in your place of work or even among your family members, it's not because of what you did wrong or something you didn't do. In fact, you may dedicate to doing the right thing and still be face with challenges. It's not about you, it's because we are in a war zone.

On the other side, this battle is not physical. Yes! It is spiritual. Apostle Paul wrote in (Ephesians 6:12 [KJV]), *"For we wrestle not against flesh and blood, but against principalities, against powers, against the rulers of the darkness of this world, against spiritual wickedness in high places."* This shows that the contention aren't with forces that can be seen, but spiritual forces. The devil is not the picture we see in movies, but spiritual. His angels, or demons aren't forces than can be seen but spiritual. That's why it's called spiritual warfare. It's not like the war between the United State and Afghanistan, not between Russia and Ukraine. It is a real battle and we must brace up for it.

Chapter 2

HOW PRECIOUS IS YOUR SOUL?

Being made in the likeness of God is the most significant attribute of man, God created all things but nothing beats man among all His creatures. It was so because the man was made just like God, the Maker. And also, the man carried the breath of God in him which signifies the very life of God. So these characteristics are what made man the most perfect and greatest creation that God made; but why do you think the devil took it heavily to fight God in order to dominate man? Perhaps because he saw the completeness in man.

Man was created dominant, he has all the attributes of God. The only One above man is God. In that same Genesis, it was recorded that man was to rule over other creatures, and bear it in mind that these other creatures exist before man, yet they don't have the beauty, qualifications and sense of belonging to compete with man.

It's a beautiful thing to know that you are created in this way, in the pattern of God, according to God's mind, beautifully and fearfully made, without limits, and so much more, in fact, (Psalms 8:4-8) gives another dimension of man, his powers and personalities, the truth is that these elements are what makes the soul of man precious that the devil had to contend with God over the soul of man. Who doesn't want good things?

The devil wanted to continue his duel with God, and the best place to stage the war was to take over God's original creature (Man). Nothing is more expensive, precious, or tangible than the soul of man. You're a superior creation, don't let anyone or anything make you inferior, in fact, you are more honorable than the angels, what else? So seek to live according to your Creator.

The Fight Began In The Spirit (Eden)

The first war between God and satan started in heaven, the host of heaven overcame Lucifer and his angels and they were cast into the earth this happened before the second war, which was a battle to overtake the soul of man.

Eden means the presence of God, where He and his children reside. The quest for superiority between God and satan still lingered till the time man was created, it was a stage for God to show that He was really superior to satan (which truly He is), so the next phase of the battle between God and satan happened in God's own turf, right in His presence, He was confident that He would win the war except that man disappointed Him by bowing to the devil.

Man's Fall From Grace

The coup started when satan saw that Eve was alone, no one knew the movement of Adam, how he had left his wife which he was to protect alone, in fact, it was a slack of duty in his path to be without the woman that was entrusted to his hands, because if Adam was with the woman, the devil wouldn't have succeeded in deceiving them.

The devil played on Eve's intelligence by telling her that if she can just eat the forbidden fruit, she would be like God. Even though they were already like God by creation. This is the greatest deceit of all time, come on, Eve and her man were already made in God's image, what else can be bigger?

But they soon forgot God's commandment, anyway it was given to the man and not the woman that was why it wasn't as in for the woman, but it became as in the moment the man ate the fruit (Genesis 3:6). The instruction was specifically and originally given to the man (Genesis2:16) and not the woman, the man was responsible; hence God was seriously annoyed.

Adam displayed another instance of negligence. He was entrusted with the responsibility to nourish and care for Eve, not the reverse. However, the moment Eve provided sustenance to Adam, contrary to God's commandments, it marked the day when the devil took control of the human soul. The apostles caution us that it is the man's duty to provide for his family, and anyone who falls short of this responsibility has denied the faith and is worse than an unbeliever (1 Timothy 5:8).

Once the devil succeeded in deceiving man through his helpmate, he gained dominance over man and since that day man has fallen out of grace; God placed curses on the man, there was total separation between the man and his Creator, from palace he became an alien to the throne, and through him, sin came to the world, and every human has this sinful skin in them.

Your Soul Is at risk

By now you should be aware that your soul is so precious than any other thing you could think of, in Matthew 16:26, Jesus was explaining to His disciples that nothing can be taken as a replacement for the soul, the soul of man is so precious hence God and satan are the real contenders. It's your choice to give it to whoever you want. For instance, the event in the garden of Eden would not have been interesting if God didn't put the forbidden fruit in the garden, it was so that God can really see the heart of man if he truly loves Him or not.

Let it be certain that no one can claim that he or she loves God, except there is a temptation or alternative to choose between someone or something else. You can boast of your love for God when you deny satan when he brings his offerings, even Jesus was not left out of those when He was on the earth, He faced temptations being tempted of the devil, the devil had to let Him go when he noticed that He was unyielding to him. My friend, you and I are not above being tempted, because the enemy wants to overtake the precious thing in your life and claim it to himself, will you give in to him? We are not the only one in this race, it had happened to the apostles, in time past, in Luke 22:31 the devil desired the soul of Peter, Jesus quickly called his attention to it nevertheless he felt for the devil but thankfully he was able to retrace his steps back to God but not everyone had this kind of grace.

What about Judas? Denied God and perished in the process, this soul of man is the battleground where the biggest fight occurs. Let me tell you that because you are alive and reading this book, then it is a sign that God still loves you and demands your soul, He is the original owner, will you hand it over to Him? Or you will let the devil win this battle again?

Hold on to Your Soul

Since Adam fell, everyone fell; God no longer reckon with man, He regretted creating man nevertheless He still wants a reunion with mankind, that's why He sent Moses, the Kings, Major and Minor Prophets, and they could not make this happen though they did their best, and overall He sent His One and only Son, Jesus Christ to reunite us with Him.

He's aware of the devices of the enemy which the devil uses, having fallen the man in Eden, God has given us another chance of winning this spiritual warfare, the only way is to surrender our lives to Him through His Son.

By accepting Jesus as your Lord and personal Savior means you say NO to satan and his deeds, you are more than a conqueror because greater is He that lives in you than he that is in the world, sin no longer have dominion over you, you have won the battle of your soul for God, heaven will indeed rejoice. Hallelujah!

Christ has come to destroy the works of satan. He did it on the cross for you and I. He claimed the biggest victory, no victory can be compared to the cross where the innocent BLOOD was shed for you and I. His blood washed away our sins and make us become God's children, reclaiming back the identity we lost in Eden, now through Christ we of Him that made us.

Your soul has been purchased with the precious blood of Jesus, you are redeemed and a Royal Priesthood, you have to constantly fight off the devices of the devil through intercessory prayer, dedicated fasting, spiritual gifts, obedience to God, intimacy with Christ, sacraments of the church, physical healing, and demonic deliverance.

So, continually fortify yourself with the Word of God so that you won't fall for the devil your enemy, your soul is for God, the devil has no part in you. The armor is your security and protection against all spiritual battles. So take your spirit man seriously. Develop a robust spirit and you continue to control all other affairs in the physical.

Chapter 3

BORN INTO SPIRITUAL WARFARE

In the previous chapter, we examined some Bible passages that shows that there is a spiritual war going on in the unseen heavenly realms here on the earth. A war that has zero regard for who you are or what you do or how much money you have or what's your status quo. And believers are usually the main target. Jesus describes salvation as being born again. He explained this truth in His conversation with Nicodemus. The Scripture says in (John 3:1-6 [KJV]), *"There was a man of the Pharisees, named Nicodemus, a ruler of the Jews: The same came to Jesus by night, and said unto him, Rabbi, we know that thou art a teacher come from God: for no man can do these miracles that thou doest, except God be with Him. Jesus answered and said unto him, verily, verily, I say unto thee, Except a man be born again, he cannot see the kingdom of God. Nicodemus saith unto Him, How can a man be born when he is old? can he enter the second time into his mother's womb, and be born? Jesus answered, Verily, verily, I say unto thee, Except a man be born of water and of the Spirit, he cannot enter into the kingdom of God. That which is born of the flesh is flesh; and that which is born of the Spirit is spirit."* Two baptisms here; one by water and one by the Spirit.

Jesus made it known from the Scripture above that salvation is like giving birth to a child. It's a birthing into a new kingdom. Remember in the previous chapter we understood that the war that broke out in heaven created two kingdoms, the kingdom of God and the kingdom of satan. We are all in the kingdom of satan, but through the sacrifice of Jesus on the cross, we died in Adam and are born into a new kingdom, the kingdom of God. The Bible says in (Colossians 1:12 [KJV]), *"Giving thanks unto the Father, which hath made us meet to be partakers of the inheritance of the saints in light: Who hath delivered us from the power of darkness, and hath translated us into the kingdom of his dear Son: In whom we have redemption through His blood, even the forgiveness of sins:"*

When we are saved, we are no longer in the kingdom of darkness but are born into the kingdom of God. We are not new babies in this new kingdom. However, at new birth, we were born into an existing battle. If you are a Christian, you should understand that you are in a spiritual battle. You are the primary target in this battle. We shouldn't believe the lie that spiritual warfare is not for everyone but some "super Christians." On the contrary, all believers are born again into an ongoing battle against the powers of darkness and sin.

War, no matter how devastating, can't stop life from taking its course. Therefore, even in times of war children are born. Christians are just like these kids, we are born into war.

The woman and the dragon

Now let's examine a fierce battle in the book of Revelations, (Revelations 12:1-6, 13-17 [NIV]), the Bible says, *"A great sign appeared in heaven: a woman clothed with the sun, with the moon under her feet and a crown of twelve stars on her head. She was pregnant and cried out in pain as she was about to give birth. Then another sign appeared in heaven: an enormous red dragon with seven heads and ten horns and seven crowns on its heads. Its tail swept a third of the stars out of the sky and flung them to the earth. The dragon stood in front of the woman who was about to give birth, so that it might devour her child the moment he was born. She gave birth to a son, a male child, who "will rule all the nations with an iron scepter." And her child was snatched up to God and to his throne. The woman fled into the wilderness to a place prepared for her by God, where she might be taken care of for 1,260 days.*

When the dragon saw that he had been hurled to the earth, he pursued the woman who had given birth to the male child. The woman was given the two wings of a great eagle, so that she might fly to the place prepared for her in the wilderness, where she would be taken care of for a time, times and half a time, out of the serpent's reach. Then from his mouth the serpent spewed water like a river, to overtake the woman and sweep her away with the torrent. But the earth helped the woman by opening its mouth and swallowing the river that the dragon had spewed out of his mouth. Then the dragon was enraged at the woman and went off to wage war against the rest of her offspring—those who keep God's commands and hold fast their testimony about Jesus."

If you read carefully you see a little child born into the welcoming mouth of a fierce dragon. The innocent woman carried the child for the full month and at the point of delivery, a dangerous dragon was waiting to devour the child. The woman was safe and in peace before the child was born. She didn't seem like a threat to the dragon for nine full months but the moment the child was born, all hell broke loose.

The Scriptures describe the dragon as the devil who was defeated by Michael and the other angels of light. The woman ran away and yet the dragon followed on. This shows how relentless satan is in this battle. He was defeated in heaven but vowed to ruin the inhabitants of the earth. The Bible say the woman's offspring was the enemy's targets. Which refers to the children of God. You and I who are born again are the devil's target. We are on his red list. He is thinking night and day how to terrorize and oppress the saints on the earth.

Jesus was born into a battle

Like the woman in the book of Revelation. We also see Jesus born of Mary into a fierce battle. The Bible says in (Matthew 2:1-5, 13-16 [KJV]), *"When Jesus was born in the village of Bethlehem in Judea, Herod was king. During this time some wise men from the east came to Jerusalem and said, "Where is the child born to be king of the Jews? We saw his star in the east and have come to worship Him." When King Herod heard about this, he was worried, and so was everyone else in Jerusalem. Herod brought together the chief priests and the teachers of the Law of Moses and asked them, "Where will the Messiah be born?" They told him, "He will be born in Bethlehem, just as the prophet wrote, After the wise men had gone, an angel from the Lord appeared to Joseph in a dream and said, "Get up! Hurry and take the child and his mother to Egypt! Stay there until I tell you to return, because Herod is looking for the child and wants to kill him." That night, Joseph got up and took his wife and the child to Egypt, where they stayed until Herod died. So the Lord's promise came true, just as the prophet had said, "I called my son out of Egypt." When Herod found out that the wise men from the east had tricked him, he was very angry. He gave orders for his men to kill all the boys who lived in or near Bethlehem and were two years old and younger. This was based on what he had learned from the wise men."*

Before Jesus was born, king Herod had peace of mind ruling the people. He felt like a good king and he didn't feel threatened or harassed. But when the wise men told him about the birth of Jesus, the Bible says he was troubled and worried. The birth of Jesus suddenly made him loose sleep. He lost his peace and for the first time he felt insecure. He felt this little child wants to take over my throne. The question is, what was Jesus' mission on the earth? Is He really here to take over from king Herod? Does Herod expect to still be alive when Jesus is old enough to be a king? Did he read somewhere that Jesus is coming to remove him from the throne and banish him from the land?

These are simple logical questions that doesn't add up. Why should Herod be troubled at the news of Jesus' birth? There is no natural answer to this question but it is only a contention of the forces of darkness. Jesus wasn't even born in a decent hospital with professional medical practitioners attending to him and Mary. He was born in a manger, yet the battle located Him. So it's not about your color or gender, anyone that is born again is a target of satan.

Herod didn't just sit by and watched the child grow, like the dragon that wanted to swallow the woman's child at the point of delivery, Herod was ready to kill Jesus even as a child. The Bible says when he lost track of the exact location of his birth, he ordered the execution of all children within Jesus' age bracket. What a massacre. The Bible says in (Matthew 2:18 [CEV]), *"In Ramah a voice was heard crying and weeping loudly. Rachel was mourning for her children, and she refused to be comforted, because they were dead."*

This verse describes a typical aftermath of war. When two nations battle against each other, the women and children are vulnerable. They are obviously can't go to war but they suffer from the aftermath which is expressed in tears and mourning. This same reaction is seen after Herod ordered the killing of innocent children, to show that it wasn't just a genocide but a warfare. The child was born and while there was joy in heaven, satan sharpened his sword and went to battle using king Herod as an excuse.

My friend, salvation is a change of state from darkness to light. You won't expect satan to fold his arm and watch you go away from his grip. That is the reason he is all out against you. You are born again on the battlefield not in a cozy waterbed.

Peter and the other disciples wouldn't have been at the forefront of contention by the Pharisee if they didn't identify with Jesus. The devil is fine with you without Christ. But the moment they chose Jesus, the radar of satan was beamed at them. The Bible says in (Acts 12:1-4 [KJV]), *"At that time King Herod caused terrible suffering for some members of the church. He ordered soldiers to cut off the head of James, the brother of John. When Herod saw that this pleased the Jewish people, he had Peter arrested during the Festival of Unleavened Bread. He put Peter in jail and ordered four squads of soldiers to guard him. Herod planned to put him on trial in public after the festival."*

Did you see that? It's not likely that Herod would have had any reason to kill James if he wasn't a disciple of Jesus. Herod was angry against the church and went ahead to arrest Peter also. He took pleasure in witnessing the flow of the blood of the saints. So, you are born into a battlefield. I'm not scaring you but been born again is an enlistment on the battlefield. If Jesus who is our perfect example was born into war, you and I aren't exception. So, spiritual warfare is not something we are trying to enter or run away from, we are born into it. But our victory is sure.

Chapter 4

A WAKEUP CALL TO SPIRITUAL WICKEDNESS

All through Scriptures, we see God's Word pointing our attention to an ongoing battle of good and evil, light and darkness, seen and unseen. For some reasons, most Christians especially those in developed nations explain out this wickedness and satan likes it that way. We tell ourselves its nothing to worry about until the devil sweeps us off our feet like the flood in the days of Noah. However, this book is a wakeup call to stay spiritually alert and be sensitive. The Bible says in (1 Thesalonians 5:6-7 [ESV]), *"So then let us not sleep, as others do, but let us keep awake and be sober. For those who sleep, sleep at night, and those who get drunk, are drunk at night."*

We are call to not sleep like others did and they paid for it. We are called to stay awake with red-eye alertness. The Scriptures is full of instances that is sufficient to make us see that life is not a funfair but a warfare. Let's examine some of these Scriptures;

(2 Corinthians 10:3-5 [NIV]) says, *"For though we live in the world, we do not wage war as the world does. The weapons we fight with are not the weapons of the world. On the contrary, they have divine power to demolish strongholds. We demolish arguments and every pretension that sets itself up against the knowledge of God, and we take captive every thought to make it obedient to Christ."* I love the tone of this verse. It says we aren't waging war as the world does. It's not a war of sword and nuclear weapon, it's a full scale spiritual battle.

Also, (1 Peter 5:8-9 [NLT]) says, *"Stay alert! Watch out for your great enemy, the devil. He prowls around like a roaring lion, looking for someone to devour. Stand firm against him, and be strong in your faith. Remember that your Christian brothers and sisters all over the world are going through the same kind of suffering you are."* In other words, you can't afford to sleep off because your great enemy is awake night and day. He is never weary neither is he ready to give up. He is like a lion looking for prey. So we can't afford to sleep off.

Psalm 91 is a plethora of the various activities of the wicked which the Bible is pointing our attention to verses 3-8 KJV says, *"For He will deliver you from the snare of the fowler and from the deadly pestilence. He will cover you with His pinions, and under His wings you will find refuge; His faithfulness is a shield and buckler. You will not fear the terror of the night, nor the arrow that flies by day, nor the pestilence that stalks in darkness, nor the destruction that wastes at noonday. A thousand may fall at your side, ten thousand at your right hand, but it will not come near you. You will only look with your eyes and see the recompense of the wicked."* It is common to see people steal at night. But here we see that there are wickedness mapped out for the entire hour of the day-at noon day, in the morning, in the dark, in the day. So we need to stay awake and alert.

I've seen God open my eyes to see the image of snake eyes in people eyes who were demonized. I always look people in their eyes to see who is really talking to me. Especially, during a deliverance service. I was once in a seminary and I saw in the spirit a witch. Crazy right? A witch studying to be a pastor came behind me to pull some of my hair. Those who practice the dark can use hair to make dolls to do wicked spiritual things to control people, place curses on them, gather information, and other ungodly things. This stuff don't just happen in other countries, it is happening right in your community, on your jobs, even amongst the people you know including family members. Wickedness is practiced behind closed doors, you are not suppose to know until the Spirit of God reveals the mysteries. Don't forget the anointing destroys the yoke! Continuing with my story of the witch learning to be a pastor at a seminary experience; earlier that week, I was sharing prophetic insight amongst a small group at the school. My thought was I should be around other godly people but don't be fooled. Test the spirit by the Spirit. As I was sharing insight this woman became more interested than others. She was asking more questions concerning spiritual gifts. It seemed odd but didn't want to make a scene until God opened my eyes to see she was a witch. Yes, you do have Christian witches. Those who confess Christian confession but behind closed doors they practice the dark arts. So, when the witch ran behind me to snag the back of my head, I knew exactly what she was doing. I ran to confront her but she disappeared in the crowd of people. I was so hot. I hate evil, especially when people disguise themselves to be an angel of light. Don't forget the devil transfigured himself into an angel of light (2 Cor. 11:14).

Let me share another situation; I was at the gym one day, and a young woman called me a goddess because of my hard work and success. She had spiritual insight because she knew something about me stood out in the spirit. I said, "No, ma'am, I am a servant of the Most High God." Every time I saw her, she would ask me personal questions. Be cautious of those who ask you a lot of personal questions. For example, she asked me, "What is your husband's name? What does your husband look like? Do you have a picture?" I knew she was gathering information to consult the guiding spirits. Don't forget Saul went to a woman who practiced divination to consult a spirit for him after God left him (1 Samuel 28:8). One day, I walked into a gym all happy, and the lady was mad full of jealousy, so I was like, hey!!! Just trying to comfort her. She came by me and swiped her hand across my stomach. Immediately, I felt pain and sickness. I warred in prayer and shared with a prayer partner to pray with me for two days. Sunday came. I didn't feel like I could make it, but I pushed through it. Elder Is at church encouraged me to push through it, just to get into the house of God to worship. God's presence will break curses off your life. Healing and deliverance from evil doing is destroyed in true worship services. This is why satan and those who hide behind him like your religious program services with no power, man being puffed up, with your fine dressed up clothes. You will be looking around at others instead of being on your face to the floor laying before the throne worshipping the Father. Once He is lifted up the Spirit of God invades the place you welcome Him into; this can be your church, home, car, outside, or where ever. Side note: You need people who can agree with you in prayer (if two or three gather together in His name, He is in the midst (Matthew 18:20)). I pressed into corporate worship. The Spirit of God fell in that place. The power of God broke that curse. I went through deliverance and preached with power. Don't think because you are anointed, a leader, pastor, babe in Christ, a child, or gifted in any way that, you are not a target for satan and his reps.

I once came across the testimony of Betty Rojugbokan, an online Inspirational writer. She wrote that in the year 1997, "I had just accepted Jesus into my heart as my Lord and Savior. And was eagerly learning the way of the Lord, studying my Bible, reading Christian books, fasting, and praying. One night, I had a dream. In that dream, I saw myself on a field, surrounded by about seven armed men coming towards me. Each of them had a machete. Meanwhile, I was singing praises to God in that dream as I was in the field. And I didn't stop singing as they approached me. Somehow, they couldn't come near me, all they did was motion for me to move in the direction they pointed.

I moved and continued singing and praising God with a loud voice till we got to the end of the field. Then I saw their leader all dressed in black waiting for me. It was at this point, I stopped singing to hear what he had to say. Then he ordered his team members to go and cut off my head with the machete. And as they made a move towards me, these exact words came out of my mouth. "But I can't die!" immediately, they stepped back from me as if struck by an unseen force and that's how I woke up. The Scripture that came to my heart when I woke up was; "I shall not die, but I shall live, and recount the deeds of the LORD. Psalms 118:17. That was 22 years ago, and God has kept me by His power till now."[4]

The truth is that it's not all things that happen around us that are natural. Behind it is the wickedness of the devil. The enemy is deliberate about oppressing the earth especially the saints. The Bible reveals that we are arrayed in battle against wicked and cruel enemies who hate humanity. There are so many things that happen in the world that are caused by demonic powers not just human activities. Therefore, our understanding of the agenda of spiritual wickedness will help us position ourselves for this fierce battle.

Friend, wickedness is real! We live in a world that is completely engulfed in wickedness. Spiritual wickedness is revealed in demonic spirits who are the architects of the heinous evil we see happening in our societies today. They aren't mere human weaknesses or greed but the work of the powers of darkness. For instance, how do you explain a male getting married to each other when even animal of same sex wouldn't mate with each other. This is no longer mere human transaction. How can a father abandon his family and move in with another woman while his children starve and drop out of school? During the civil war in Liberia, two rebels would see a pregnant woman walking and start an argument regarding the gender of the foetus. To solve their misunderstanding, they will open the woman's stomach and kill the innocent woman and her unborn child.[5]

We have heard of different terrorist groups on TV who viciously behead innocent people and take over communities on an unprecedented scale. These and many more are acts conducted by demonic entities. The war between Russia and Ukraine is not between Russians president Putin's forces and the Ukrainians, rather, the real forces involved in this warfare are wicked spirits. And until these wicked forces are dealt with in the realm of the spirit, the physical, political, economically strategies by nations around the world can only provide temporary mitigation. It is like trying to fight satan with guns, RPGs, or even nuclear weapons.

Most sicknesses and diseases today aren't just due to stress but are works of the devil to oppress people. Most of the healings that our Lord Jesus effected, He confronted and dealt with the spirit behind the sickness and the problem was rectified. The Bible talks about an incident when a boy was brought to Jesus for healing.

In our days we may have advised that the parents should take him to see a psychiatric doctor perhaps it's just a slight mental illness.

But see Jesus' response in (Mark 9:25-27 [CEV]), *"When Jesus saw that a crowd was gathering fast, he spoke sternly to the evil spirit that had kept the boy from speaking or hearing. He said, "I order you to come out of the boy! Don't ever bother him again." The spirit screamed and made the boy shake all over. Then it went out of him. The boy looked dead, and almost everyone said he was. But Jesus took hold of his hand and helped him stand up."* Jesus spoke to the devil responsible for that sickness and ordered them out of the boy. People say the boy misbehaving but no one saw the spirits tormenting him.

Also, there was a woman who had an ailment that defied medical procedures. You can imagine loosing blood for twelve full years without any physical injury? The Bible says in (Mark 5:24-29 [CEV]), *"Jesus went with Jairus. Many people followed along and kept crowding around. In the crowd was a woman who had been bleeding for twelve years. She had gone to many doctors, and they had not done anything except cause her a lot of pain. She had paid them all the money she had. But instead of getting better, she only got worse. The woman had heard about Jesus, so she came up behind him in the crowd and barely touched His clothes. She had said to herself, "If I can just touch his clothes, I will get well." As soon as she touched them, her bleeding stopped, and she knew she was well."* Nothing could heal her except the power of light in Jesus that dispelled the power of darkness responsible for her pain.

My friend, please, it's time to stop seeing these events as mere humans' operations and let's address the real cause of the problem. It's time to come awake. I love this hymn by Charlotte Elliott (1836), titled *"Christian, seek not yet repose."*

> *"Christian, seek not yet repose,*
> *Cast thy dreams of ease away;*
> *Thou art in the midst of foes:*
> *Watch and pray.*
> *Principalities and pow'rs,*
> *Must'ring their unseen array,*
> *Wait for thine unguarded hours:*
> *Watch and pray.*
> *Gird thy heav'nly armor on,*
> *Wear it ever, night and day;*
> *Ambushed lies the evil one:*
> *Watch and pray."[6]*

This is a call to wake up from slumber and fight. If we watch satan take over, we may keep groaning, but we need to see events from the standpoint of the spirit not just the physical. Some families are struggling with marital delay and they keep going from one makeup artist to another so they can look good. It's okay to look good, but contend with the forces behind the delay. We have churches that have lost the fire of God and nothing supernatural happens there anymore. It's time to wake up, Oh man of God and see that we are in a wicked world.

The Scripture says in (Psalm 74:20 [ISV]), *"Pay attention to your covenant, for the dark regions of the earth are full of violence.*" You may have been a victim in the past but it's time to be aware. That hymn says please don't seek rest, cast away the thought of being at ease because you are in the midst of your arch enemies. So, stay awake and see that no natural effect has a natural cause.

Chapter 5

THE KEY OF SPIRITUAL KNOWLEDGE

A military personnel would never attempt going to battle without a battle plan. What is a battle plan? It's a strategy to exploit your enemies' weaknesses and to maximize your strengths so you can win.[7] It involves gathering information about both your adversaries and the area you are navigating. Failure to explore this knowledge could endanger the lives of well-prepared soldiers. So, it's not about preparing for war, but we need the knowledge of who we are going against if we must return in one piece from any battle.

Sun Tzu wrote in his book *The Art of War*, "If you know the enemy and know yourself, you need not fear the result of a hundred battles."[8] In other words, the place of knowledge in defeating the opponents in any battle cannot be over emphasized. Even in football, the coach come in to the team and prepares them based on the knowledge of their opponents. They check the team they are playing against and observe their strategies and their pattern of play in the previous matches. From that knowledge, the coach prepares his team appropriately to win the tournament.

Jay Shetty once said, "Knowledge is power, and it can help you overcome any fear of the unexpected. When you learn, you gain more awareness through the process, and you know what pitfalls to look for as you get ready to transition to the next level."[9] Like physical war which requires knowledge of how the opponent thinks and operates, we also need the knowledge of how our enemy thinks if we must be victorious at all times.

May I quickly say that satan doesn't give up. Yes, he comes again and again. The Bible says about Jesus in (Luke 4:13 [ESV]), *"And when the devil had ended every temptation, he departed from Him until an opportune time."* This was after the battle in the wilderness. The Scripture says the devil left Him until another opportune time. What does that imply? The battle is never ending. The devil only leaves the battlefield to refuel. You may have won at some point, but understand that he is around the corner. And he won't come to you in the same form like the previous time. He comes in different shades and forms. So we need to be fully aware of all his tactics else our victory would be once upon a time.

We need to know how the enemy comes and be able to discern his craftiness. He doesn't always come at us through obvious means. He is crafty. He schemes. So we need to develop spiritual intelligence to know when the enemy is manifesting and how to stop him. One important component of warfare is knowledge or intelligence. You can't go into battle without adequate knowledge of your enemy. The enemy has weapons and strategies that we must understand if we will overcome his assaults. The Bible says in (2 Corinthians 2:11 [CEV]), *"I have done this to keep satan from getting the better of us. We all know what goes on in his mind."* Ignorance is his devices and its the sure way to defeat.

The devil doesn't come at us with ugly looks but he now blends into the natural features of our environment- our culture, art, and into different aspects of our society. This camouflage makes it increasingly difficult for the church to spot and root him out. This makes knowledge become a decisive factor in spiritual warfare.

This war is not to get a person's things or wealth, the devil uses our things to get to the ultimate goal, which is our soul. The devil wants the person's soul in eternal hell. I remember one Sunday in church. I was praying just from knowledge praying before service. God's voice intervene and said to me stop praying and pick up your prayer book in your bag which was a spiritual warfare book and start praying it instead of your prayer. I was like I can't stop praying now it will not look good in the middle of prayer service amongst the people. It'll interrupt the flow of the service.

Sadly, I continued to pray my way and shortly after it was like I couldn't speak anymore. It was like (Luke 1:20-25) when John's father couldn't speak until John was born. I looked at the church people and confessed what God had told me. I obeyed then started praying the warfare prayers. It opened the Heavens over the church. Miracles and signs started happening. Spiritual gifts was activated within the people. Visions and spiritual ears opened. God was showing me the enemy was present. Oh I didn't mention that I also heard the devil speak. He said to me, "You can grow the largest church here. You all can praise your God and fall on the floor, but I have a problem with you when you snatch people out of my hands!" Wow, you can still be praising God and still be in satan's hands.

The Scripture says in (Hosea 4:6 [ESV]), *"My people are destroyed for lack of knowledge; because you have rejected knowledge, I reject you from being a priest to me. And since you have forgotten the law of your God, I also will forget your children."* Did you see that? The saints are destroyed because they lack knowledge. In other words, they become prey to the enemy because they have no knowledge of how he operates. The Bible went further to say that actually, they rejected the knowledge. This is unfortunate. I've come to realize that satan doesn't have a problem when we sing and dance, but he has a problem with our understanding of who we are in Christ, and the victory we have in redemption. He knows that nothing sends him off our back faster than our knowledge of God's Word.

It is written

Now let's examine how Jesus overcame His first public contention against satan. After John baptized Jesus in Jordan river, He was led by the Spirit to the wilderness and He was there for forty full days. The Bible says in (Luke 4:1-13 [ERV]), *"Now filled with the Holy Spirit, Jesus returned from the Jordan River. And then the Spirit led Him into the desert. There the devil tempted Jesus for 40 days. Jesus ate nothing during this time, and when it was finished, He was very hungry. The devil said to Him, "If you are the Son of God, tell this rock to become bread." Jesus answered, "The Scriptures say, 'It is not just bread that keeps people alive.'" Then the devil took Jesus and in a moment of time showed Him all the kingdoms of the world. The devil said to Him, "I will make you king over all these places. You will have power over them, and you will get all the glory. It has all been given to me. I can give it to anyone I want.*

I will give it all to you, if you will only worship me." Jesus answered, "The Scriptures say, 'You must worship the Lord your God. Serve only Him.'" Then the devil led Jesus to Jerusalem and put Him on a high place at the edge of the Temple area. He said to Him, "If you are the Son of God, jump off! The Scriptures say, 'God will command His angels to take care of you.' It is also written, 'Their hands will catch you so that you will not hit your foot on a rock.'" Jesus answered, "But the Scriptures also say, 'You must not test the Lord your God.'" The devil finished tempting Jesus in every way and went away to wait until a better time."

Jesus had just completed forty days of intense fellowship and empowerment of the Spirit. You will expect that the angels would rush at Him and ordinate Him for ministry like we do for new ministers. But no, satan was first. He stepped in and began a series of deceptive conversation with Jesus.

Friend, the first knowledge you need is that satan is deceptive. Deception is a strategy of satan. I find people doing good things for others in need. We are deceived by their good doing until God reveal the hidden spirit behind the puppet. He came to Jesus and started like he cared. Of course Jesus was hungry and that was where the battle began. "Turn this stones to bread." You don't need to starve unnecessarily when you have the power. Aren't you the Son of God? Jesus replied, it is written. He come again with another enticing offer. Yet, Jesus replied, it is written.

The question is how much of what is written do you know? How much of God's Word do you have loaded in your spirit? Apostle Paul writes in (Colossians 3:16 [NIV]), *"Let the Word of Christ dwell in you richly as you teach and admonish one another with all wisdom, and as you sing psalms, hymns and spiritual songs with gratitude in your hearts to God."* He emphasized that the Word should be seated in you abundantly. Imagine that Jesus had the Word sparingly in His Spirit, how would He respond to the second and the third missile thrown at Him? Yes, He shut the devil up the first time, but the battle is not over. So, we need to allow God's Word to dwell richly in us to be able to overcome the scheme of

satan. The devil comes to deceive the saints from following and believing Christ. So you need to be smarter if
you must overcome.

Another scheme of satan is manipulation. To manipulate means to control something or someone to their
advantage, often unfairly or dishonestly:[10] The devil
always wants to have people do the wrong thing so he
twist the truth into a lie. So, we need spiritual discern-
ment, testing the spirit to know what is true. The Bible
says in (Matthew 10:16 [KJV]), *"Behold, I send you forth
as sheep in the midst of wolves: be ye therefore wise as serpents, and harmless as doves."* So we need to know when
we are led in the wrong direction. He also emphasized in
(Matthew 7:15-20 [NIV]), *"Watch out for false prophets.
They come to you in sheep's clothing, but inwardly they are
ferocious wolves. By their fruit you will recognize them. Do
people pick grapes from thorn bushes, or figs from thistles?
Likewise, every good tree bears good fruit, but a bad tree
bears bad fruit. A good tree cannot bear bad fruit, and a
bad tree cannot bear good fruit. Every tree that does not
bear good fruit is cut down and thrown into the fire. Thus,
by their fruit you will recognize them."*

He is manipulative and always wants to drag us away
from the way of life. Jesus said we shouldn't be carried
away with people's title especially in the church, but we
should check out for the fruits they bear. They may look
white outside but dark and deadly inside.

Furthermore, satan comes at us through financial
gain. The Bible says in (Mark 8:36-37 [KJV]), *"For what*

shall it profit a man, if he shall gain the whole world, and lose his own soul? Or what shall a man give in exchange for his soul?" The devil comes to present precious offers to us like He did to Jesus. He told Jesus to bow down and worship Him so He can handover the entire riches of the earth to Him. Ah! How many times have we also fallen to this trap, or are you presently in this trap? Perhaps you have sold your soul for promotion or satan is negotiating for your soul for fame. It's time to pause and ponder.

"But it's my boss that is telling me about the offer not satan." "It's my friend that is introducing the opportunity to me not the enemy." You need to look beyond the boss sitting in that chair and see satan calling you into destruction. It's time to say no. That job that would take you away from church, or make you spend more time outside of God is not from God but from satan. That opportunity that would stop you from attending to your family and fellowshipping with the saints is satan calling your soul. It's time to say no. He presents riches just to get your soul. It's a battle and your soul is his ultimate target. Fight for it.

Lastly, you need to understand how the mind operates. The enemy always try to fill our minds with doubts, fear, and uncertainty about the future so we can sway from the faith. Diana write in her post, "The battle within our minds is one of the most important factors that must be kept in check with God's Word. While satan cannot read our minds, he can influence our thoughts. Thus, begins the race to lose or win against the battle of the mind!"[11] This knowledge helps us to guard our mind with all diligence so we don't wander away from the path of life.

So, pay attention to God's Word. Paul told his disciple in (1 Timothy 4:13-16 [NIV]), *"Until I come, devote yourself to the public reading of Scripture, to preaching and to teaching. Do not neglect your gift, which was given you through prophecy when the body of elders laid their hands on you. Be diligent in these matters; give yourself wholly to them, so that everyone may see your progress. Watch your life and doctrine closely. Persevere in them, because if you do, you will save both yourself and your hearers.*

Pay attention to the Word so you can know how satan thinks and how to avoid him. The Bible is filled with his schemes. The Bible contains our battle plan to know how to dodge the missiles of evil forces in the battle of life.

Chapter 6

THE NATURE OF OUR WARFARE

Are you familiar with the idiom, "bring a knife to a gunfight"? It paints a quite perilous picture for the guy with the knife doesn't it? This phrase means to be poorly prepared for a situation. Just as a soldier can be poorly prepared for natural warfare by bringing a knife to a gunfight, you can be inadequately prepared for spiritual warfare. That's why you have to understand the nature of the believer's warfare.

The nature of spiritual warfare means it's characteristics and features. What does this warfare look like especially from your standpoint. In natural warfare, you understand the enemy's weapons and you match him fire for fire. If he's using guns, tanks, grenades, ships and airstrikes you do the same and even more. You predict the kind of assault the enemy would launch and you strategize. All these pertain to the nature of the war going on.

In truth, the way soldiers of a city under siege fight their enemies is different from a head to head clash between two enemy armies. Therefore, the nature of the war you're involved in determines how you fight. So what's the nature of the spiritual warfare you're a part of? How can you fight effectively? What's the enemy's weapon? Taking the time to answer these questions will mean the difference between defeat and victory.

Fighting The Wrong Way

The nature of the war determines how the soldier fights. Sadly, many believers who are actively involved in spiritual warfare don't know it's true nature. This ignorance leads to ineffectiveness and defeat in their individual lives. The devil is tireless and consistent. Daily, he tries to catch you off guard and gain the upper hand. If you don't know the nature of your warfare, you won't know how to fight and win.

When you study the New Testament, it's clear that satan keeps throwing all that he's got at believers. Yet, God's Word teaches that you can overcome the devil at every turn. The Bible calls you an overcomer. (1 John 5: 4 [KJV]) says, *"For whatsoever is born of God overcometh the world...*Your victory over the devil and every other enemy to your success is assured when you know how to fight this war.

However, before discussing the right way to fight, let's talk about the wrong way. A ton of Christians are trying to get delivered from satan's power and wrestle him to the ground. They are looking for an experience outside the finished work of Christ—something more powerful than the death, burial and resurrection of Christ—that will get satan off their backs and out of their lives. Their opinion about themselves is that satan has them in chains and is in control of their whole lives. So they are trying to wrestle their way out of satan's grip.

But the Bible doesn't teach this mindset about spiritual warfare. Most people have family history and records to show satan's masterful work in their families. They believe he got their parents and siblings, and they are next. Now, if you tell them otherwise, they will show you patterns that are also playing out in their lives. "The same thing happened to my parents," they'll say. They believe satan is winning already, but have sliver of hope that God can look down from heaven and rescue them. If you're in this boat, it's the wrong way to approach spiritual warfare.

What Wrestling Truly Means

(Ephesians 6:12 [CEV]) says *"We are not fighting against humans. We are fighting against forces and authorities and against rulers of darkness and powers in the spiritual world."* Rev. Kenneth E, Hagin wrote in his book, *The Triumphant Church*: "One of the meanings of the word 'wrestle" in W.E Vine's Expository Dictionary of Biblical Words is to sway. If we will let him, the enemy will come against us and try to sway us and get us out of faith and into doubt and unbelief about the Word so he can defeat us. But if we stand our ground in faith, he cannot sway us from the Word. Therefore, the "wrestling" we do is not fighting the devil, but it is a fight sometimes to hold fast to our faith in God's Word."[12]

With the above Spirit-inspired words, Rev. Hagin explained excellently, the nature of our warfare. The word "wrestle" can throw a person off balance and get them thinking they have to struggle with satan and his cohorts to forcefully gain their freedom. But no, the enemy is only trying to shift us from the position of what Christ has already done. The truth is, Christ has already fought with the enemy and defeated them. All believers partake in His victory. We fight spiritual warfare by standing on what the Bible says Christ has done.

(Hebrews 2:14-15 [CEV]) says, *"Therefore, since the children share in flesh and blood, he likewise shared in their humanity, so that through death he could destroy the one who holds the power of death (that is, the devil), and set free those who were held in slavery all their lives by their fear of death."*

The Amplified Bible in (Colossians 2:15) says, *"When He had disarmed the rulers and authorities [those supernatural forces of evil operating against us], He made a public example of them [exhibiting them as captives in His triumphal procession], having triumphed over them through the cross."*

The Scriptures above show that the enemy has been thoroughly dealt with. He is a defeated foe. Nevertheless, satan knows that Christians can be tricked out of their victor-status. One major tool he uses is lies, and once you believe satan's lies you fall into his trap. The enemy is in the business of creating false evidence.

He will try to convince you that God lied about your protection, healing, salvation and more. He'll do these by showing you the fact of your circumstances or past experience. However, God's Word and promises are greater than fact; they are reality. If you can only stand on God's Word without swaying or wavering, the natural fact will give way to the reality of God's Word.

Freed And Delivered

Many believers are defeated and downtrodden because they are looking for what's not lost. They believe the enemy's report more than God's report. If they read in God's Word that they are healed, they'll doubt. Instead, they'll readily believe the doctor who says they have cancer and will surely die. Most Christians are bound and under satan's power because they rejected the deliverance Christ wrought on the cross. More than two millenia ago, Jesus made you and I free on the cross. You can't get any freer than that, Hallelujah! satan only takes advantage of your ignorance.

(Colossians 1:13 [KJV]) says God has, *"...delivered us from the power of darkness, and hath translated us into the kingdom of his dear Son."* The Bible refers to satan's power or kingdom as the power of darkness. Every Christian who believes in Jesus as Lord and Savior have been delivered. It's an established truth about yourself you can't change.

You no longer have to live under the power of the enemy, unless through sin or ignorance, you submit to his influence. If more believers would come to this knowledge, believers will experience more victory in their individual lives. God Himself has delivered you—set you free—from satan's power. If you will cash-in on the truth of God's Word, it'll become your experience.

(Galatians 5:1[CEV]) is another Scripture that captures the truth of your freedom. *"Christ has set us free! This means we are really free. Now hold on to your freedom and don't ever become slaves of the Law again."*

It's a fact that you've been set free—released from slavery—to sin's power, but there's still a possibility of being entangled again with the yoke of bondage. The enemy knows this, and would love nothing more than seeing you back in chains. So more than ever, you must be aware of your freedom and lay hold of it.

Beyond The Battle

Spiritual warfare is not about getting free or delivered, it's about maintaining your freedom and deliverance. The enemy already knows he's lost, Christ defeated him. Still, he relentlessly fights you, counting on either your unbelief or ignorance.

The nature of your warfare is about where you wage your war from. The devil knows that the moment you try to fight for victory, you've lost. God's people aren't fighting for a victory Jesus gave us on a platter of gold. We fight from victory. We are the army sent to trample on serpents and scorpions—the occupying army that retains the victory Christ won for us until He returns in glory.

Have you ever heard the phrase, "beyond the battle?" That's your status in this warfare. Christ already fought the battle of the ages. He's dislodged the enemy from your life and He has no place. Right now, your job is to keep him out. (Romans 8:37 [NIV]) says, *"No, in all these things we are more than conquerors through Him who loved us."* You are more than a conqueror because Christ has taken you beyond the battle. Fight from this vantage point and you'll never lose.

Here's another remarkable Scripture that reveals the nature of our warfare. (1 John 5:4 [KJV]), *For whatsoever is born of God overcometh the world and this is the victory that overcometh the world, even our faith."* Do you know what's so incredible about this Scripture? It seems to imply that God made you undefeatable when you became His offspring. You are born to overcome and triumph over all the weapons and obstacles the enemy throws at you.

Having the right understanding is crucial in spiritual warfare. A person who lacks understanding would blame God for making them a prey to such a terrible enemy. But the prudent believer will clearly see that God has set them up for victory at every turn.

Something else you should note in the previous verse is the line which reads, *"this is the victory that overcometh the world, even our faith.* The Christian life of faith is based on the victory Jesus won for you. The fuel that powers your Christian walk is the victory of Jesus, not defeat. If you would lay hold on it anytime the devil tries to assault and sway you, you'll come out unscathed and unharmed.

The devil is indeed a formidable foe, for unbelievers who don't know God. But he's a defeated foe for those who depend on Jesus and trust Him for victory. Your adversary cannot win until you leave the sphere of faith and walk with him down unbelief-avenue. You are hedged about and only vulnerable to the enemy when you start doubting God's protection. This is why faith is a vital ingredient in your spiritual warfare.

Don't let the enemy set the tone or determine how you fight through his mind games. Yes, he will try to manipulate the circumstances, your body and emotions to make you feel vulnerable and hopeless. But your advantage is not carnal but spiritual. Go into spiritual warfare wielding victory as a weapon. Stop seeing victory as a destination your trying to reach. Victory is your reality and what guarantees your success.

As God's children, we don't fight because we hope to win. Instead, we fight because we have won. Many things that Jesus accomplished on the cross on our behalf only need our participation and acceptance. Once we agree with God concerning our reality, every contrary circumstance fades out.

Those who don't understand the nature of the war they fight will fear and fidget at the thought of the enemy. But now you're among the ranks of fearless kingdom warriors and soldiers who will march into battle in their daily lives, not only to fight but to win countless victories against our defeated foe. All you need to do is remember who already won the battle for you and your more-than-conqueror status. You are fighting from victory.

Chapter 7

GIVE NO PLACE

One good news about Jesus victory on the cross of Calvary is that He defeated satan and his hold on believers. We are redeemed into a life of victory. But that victory comes at a cost. The enemy has no legal ground to oppress and suppress a child of God, unless a believer forfeits his or her place. Yes, God has equipped us to put satan in his place and keep him out of our lives, but we have a part to play to keep things that way.

We don't have to fall prey to the devil's scheme if we diligently shut every door in our lives, close all windows, and seal up every place through which the enemy would attempt to access us. In other words, Jesus handed over the door of our victory to us, which implies that we can prevent satan from meddling with the affairs of our lives.

The Bible says in (Ephesians 4:27 [KJV]), *"Neither give place to the devil."* The word "place" is the Greek word meaning "topos." It refers to a specific, geographical location, region, zone or territory.[13] This implies that the enemy is after every region of our lives. He is not impressed when we defeat him in one aspect, he tries us in another way- health, relationship marriage, money, business, emotion, ministry among others. He wants to take over every hinge and square of our lives, but he needs to first gain access and from that entry point so he can unleash his agenda in our lives.

He doesn't rest neither does he give up, so the Bible calls us to be cautious and not live carelessly else we be entangled again with sin. Paul wrote to the church in (Galatians 5:1 [KJV]), *"Stand fast therefore in the liberty wherewith Christ hath made us free, and be not entangled again with the yoke of bondage."* This is a clarion call to all believers not to give place to satan in our lives. If we give satan one tiny space to occupy, he will seize the opportunity take control of our lives. So we have a responsibility to take our place. We need to rest in the strength of the Spirit and keep pressing.

In the book of Judges, Gideon had only 300 soldiers to fight a battle against innumerable army of the Midianites. But one truth we learned from that experience is that every soldier stood in their place before God. No wonder God gave them victory. The Bible says in (Judges 7:16-21[NKJV]), *"Then he divided the three hundred men into three companies, and he put a trumpet into every man's hand, with empty pitchers, and torches inside the pitchers. And he said to them, "Look at me and do likewise; watch, and when I come to the edge of the camp you shall do as* I do: *When I blow the trumpet, I and all who are with me, then you also blow the trumpets on every side of the whole camp, and say, 'The sword of the Lord and of Gideon!'" So Gideon and the hundred men who were with him came to the outpost of the camp at the beginning of the middle watch, just as they had posted the watch; and they blew the trumpets and broke the pitchers that were in their hands. Then the three companies blew the trumpets and broke the pitchers — they held the torches in their left hands and the trumpets in their right hands for blowing — and they cried, "The sword of the Lord and of Gideon!" And every man stood in his place all around the camp; and the whole army ran and cried out and fled."*

They stood in their place without shifting grounds, so their enemy didn't have a place to occupy among them. They didn't break their ranks but were firm on their position. The Bible says in (1 Peter 5.8-9 [KJV]), *"Be sober, be vigilant; because your adversary the devil, as a roaring lion, walketh about, seeking whom he may devour: Whom resist steadfast in the faith, knowing that the same afflictions are accomplished in your brethren that are in the world."* Again, the Scripture is calling us to be steadfast and resolute.

Ways We Give Place To The Enemy

1. Sinful compromise

We are at a time when we take sin for granted. We coat it and call it weakness, trend and all sort of names. The devil creeps subtly into our society and we gently open the door for him to settle. (Songs of Solomon 2:15 [KJV]) puts it this way, *"Take us the foxes, the little foxes, that spoil the vines: for our vines have tender grapes."*

The Bible called them little foxes that looks harmless but eventually spoil our vine. They mess up our faith and before long, we have lost the battle to the devil. (Ecclesiastes 10:8 [ESV]), says, *"He who digs a pit will fall into it, and a serpent will bite him who breaks through a wall."* We have a responsibility to keep the hedge around our lives ever fortified and strong. It may look like everything is calm on the other side, but we see that the serpent is permanently at the other side. He is waiting to see an entry through that hedge. He is full of venom and wants to bite. So, we need to keep off and ensure that the hedge around us is strong and fortified.

For instance, we saw one of Jesus' close disciples, Judas Iscariot. He was chosen by Jesus after hours in prayer. Out of all the people around, He had only twelve slots and so you would expect that they are the best choice. They had a future of becoming apostles after Jesus. Jesus even promised them thrones in His Father's kingdom where they would become judges. But what happened to Judas? The Bible says in (John 12:6 [CEV]), *"Judas did not really care about the poor. He asked this because he carried the moneybag and sometimes would steal from it."* Judas was an executive member of Jesus' cabinet. He was the chief financial controller and financial auditor. That sounds like a top management position, isn't it? But Judas lowered the edge. He started to compromise and stole from the business account. It didn't matter when He stole because he felt good. He was still going out with Jesus and praying for people. But he already gave a place to satan through those acts.

Eventually he lost his position and his life. Remember, satan want to take the whole place. We used to think we could contain him behind closed doors where no one would see him, but unfortunately, he always finds his way out. So, it's better you send that devil out before he takes over your life. He is nor merciful in anyway, his agenda is to ultimately destroy. I pray you shall not be destroyed, in Jesus name. Peter denied Jesus, but took back and won the battle. But Judas lost the battle to satan and everything that matter.

What about a couple in the early church named Ananias and Sapphira. They were also devoted believers under the teaching of Peter. But they also allowed a little compromise into their lives and that was it.

The Bibles says in (Act 5:1-10 [CEV]), *"Ananias and his wife Sapphira also sold a piece of property. But they agreed to cheat and keep some of the money for themselves. So when Ananias took the rest of the money to the apostles, Peter said, "Why has satan made you keep back some of the money from the sale of the property? Why have you lied to the Holy Spirit? The property was yours before you sold it, and even after you sold it, the money was still yours. What made you do such a thing? You didn't lie to people. You lied to God!" As soon as Ananias heard this, he dropped dead, and everyone who heard about it was frightened. Some young men came in and wrapped up his body. Then they took it out and buried it. Three hours later Sapphira came in, but she did not know what had happened to her husband. Peter asked her, "Tell me, did you sell the property for this amount?" "Yes," she answered, "that's the amount." Then Peter said, "Why did the two of you agree to test the Lord's Spirit? The men who buried Ananias are by the door, and they will carry you out!" At once she fell at Peter's feet and died. When the young men came back in, they found Sapphira lying there dead. So, they carried her out and buried her beside her husband."*

They felt it could be business as usual but this time they lost it. Judas also played with the serpents' head for a while before he finally got bitten. Friend, take your hand and put away those sinful compromise. Whatever the Bible calls sin should remain sin to you. Avoid rationalizing it and keep following Jesus. He has laid God's way for living life.

2. Walking in the flesh

The Bible says in (Galatians 3:1-5 [CEV]), *"You stupid Galatians! I told you exactly how Jesus Christ was nailed to a cross. Has someone now put an evil spell on you? I want to know only one thing. How were you given God's Spirit? Was it by obeying the Law of Moses or by hearing about Christ and having faith in Him? How can you be so stupid? Do you think that by yourself you can complete what God's Spirit started in you? Have you gone through all of this for nothing? Is it all really for nothing? God gives you His Spirit and works miracles in you. But does He do this because you obey the Law of Moses or because you have heard about Christ and have faith in Him?"*

These were people that Paul preached to about Christ and even established them in a fellowship. But after some time, they allowed flesh into their midst. Paul said they started on the Spirit and felt they could continue in the flesh. That's a no. The Bible says in (Romans 13:13-14 [ERV]), *"We should live in a right way, like people who belong to the day. We should not have wild parties or be drunk. We should not be involved in sexual sin or any kind of immoral behavior. We should not cause arguments and trouble or be jealous. But be like the Lord Jesus Christ, so that when people see what you do, they will see Christ. Don't think about how to satisfy the desires of your sinful self."* satan draws us gradually to engage in the things of the flesh and we say *"it doesn't matter."* He may even give us Scriptures to justify it. Paul knew the end of such a lifestyle that's why he shouted at the Galatians.

Friend, allow Jesus to remain your Lord and allow His ways to remain your ways. Content for a life of the Spirit by all means. Don't let satan steal you from the way. No matter the pressures around, let your life remain in the Spirit, patterned after the dictates of Scriptures and not social media trends.

3. Relationships.

There is a popular saying that "Show me your friend and I'll tell you who you are"[14] We are not far from the company we keep. The Scripture says in (1 Corinthians 15:33 [NCV]), *"Do not be fooled: "Bad friends will ruin good habits."* When satan can't reach us directly, he positions people with bad intentions across our path. You hear people say, "My friends said it's okay, so I agreed?"

Many people have found themselves in trouble because they followed their friend's advice. Who do you surround yourself with? Are they godly people or those that do not know they Lord? It's time to do an audit of our relationships else we would lose the battle of life. Who are you desiring to get married to? Are Scriptural principle the bedrock of your relationship or just because they are handsome, wealthy and influential. Friend, be deliberate about your relationships. We have seen great men of God who lost their calling and ministry, jobs, family and children because of the spouse they married or the friends they kept.

The Scripture talks about the story of Amon in (2 Samuel 13:1-5 [NIV]), *"In the course of time, Amnon son of David fell in love with Tamar, the beautiful sister of Absalom son of David. Amnon became frustrated to the point of illness on account of his sister Tamar, for she was a virgin, and it seemed impossible for him to do anything to her. Now Amnon had a friend named Jonadab son of Shimeah, David's brother. Jonadab was a very shrewd man. He asked Amnon, "Why do you, the king's son, look so haggard morning after morning? Won't you tell me?" Amnon said to him, "I'm in love with Tamar, my brother Absalom's sister." "Go to bed and pretend to be ill," Jonadab said. "When your father comes to see you, say to him, 'I would like my sister Tamar to come and give me something to eat. Let her prepare the food in my sight so I may watch her and then eat it from her hand.'"*

This was satan planting an evil friend around the son of David and it led to his death and a permanent enmity among David's children. Absalom eventually planned the death of Amnon after two years. You can imagine how such innocent advice ruined a happy family. Why? satan gain entrance through a bad relationship. Are you a parents? Be careful about the relationships your children keep. Watch your spouse's relationship because their advice may open the door for satan into your marriage.

4. Our Emotion (Anger)

Anger is one emotion that we explain away which satan uses to penetrate our gate. Some people give excuse that they are human and should be angry when they want to be angry. That's true, but how do you manage this emotion? The Bible warns in (Ephesians 4:26-27, [NIV]), *"In your anger do not sin," Do not let the sun go down while you are still angry, and do not give the devil a foothold.* So, anger is one of satan's access points into our lives. Usually, anger leads to offence towards the people we are angry at if we allow it to linger.

Rick Renner once shared an experience he had with one of his employees. He said, "I received information about one department of our ministry that really upset me. What upset me even more was that I believed one of our employees had known about this problem but hadn't conveyed the full truth to me about it. I scheduled a meeting to talk to that person the next morning to discuss this situation. That night as I lay in bed, I began to think about the problem we were facing. The longer I thought about it, the more angry I became that I hadn't been fully informed about the details as I should have been. I could feel a flash of heat pass through me as I kept pondering what to do next.

As I lay there in that bed, I began to take up an offense with this leader in our ministry. Once the devil got that foothold in my mind and emotions, it was as if a door had suddenly swung wide open for the devil to come in and begin accusing and slandering that precious employee to me. I tossed and turned all night long. I knew I could lay this issue down and walk in peace, or I could let it build in my mind until I became a walking time bomb. I chose to hold on to it and let it fester throughout the night.

The next morning when our meeting began, I exploded! My thinking was so distorted by the devil's ravings in my mind all night that I couldn't hear anything being said. I was livid with this employee. This employee couldn't even say anything, as I never even gave her ten seconds to respond to my accusations.

Later when the whole ordeal was over, I discovered that every detail of the problem had already been fully communicated to me. But I had been so busy at the time that I didn't even remember the conversation. Others on the staff remembered it very well. It was my fault that I didn't know and not hers.

I was so embarrassed that I had lost my temper. I asked my staff members for forgiveness, and they were spiritual enough to forgive me and allow me to be a man with real human frailties. Thank God, our long-term relationship and commitment to work as a team overrides moments of human weakness that all of us display at one time or another."[15]

When we are angry satan starts to secretly penetrate our minds and emotions and in the process, a wedge is driven between us and those we are angry at. His objective is to separate us and make us live in hate instead of love. At the point of anger, our perspective about the other person suddenly changes from positive to negative and we start to generate faults in their actions. This is clear evidence that satan has found an entry point into our minds and our lives. Friend, don't allow those negative emotions or disagreement to linger, settle it right now and move on in love.

5. Unforgiveness

The devil like to amplify peoples fault and make it look like that's the worst and so we keep withdrawing the hand of forgiveness. It's time to quit meditating on all the bad points and wrongs and see them through the mirror of love. Consider how many times you've let down other people; how many mistakes you've made in your relationships; the times you should have been held accountable but instead were shown unbelievable mercy. Remembering these things has a way of making you look at an offensive situation a little more mercifully. Jesus said in (Matthew 6:12, 15 [NKJV]), *"And forgive us our debts, as we forgive our debtors. But if you do not forgive men their trespasses, neither will your Father forgive your trespasses."*

If we don't forgive people their sins, God would also not forgive us our sins. The enemy knows this, hence he tries to push us against people and tags their faults as unforgivable. Unforgiveness is the cheapest way to be separated from God. And when we are drawn away from God, we are welcome into satan's evil hand. So fight that thoughts that wants to keep you in unforgiveness. Don't open that door for satan.

Jesus discouraged living in unforgiveness in (Matt 18:21-22 [TLB]) when Peters opened the conversation. The Bible says, *"Then Peter came to Him and asked, "Sir, how often should I forgive a brother who sins against me? Seven times?" "No!" Jesus replied, "seventy times seven!"* This is a simple way of saying don't hold on to anything. Don't hold on to any offence. Let it go completely and let God have His way in your heart.

Yes, it may be difficult at times, that's why we have the Holy Spirit to help us stay awake. Ask Him to help you let it go. Pray to God to help you forgive that person you are holding bound. He is there to help you fight the battle and overcome. Check out my book, "Let Them Go!" A Christian Guide on the Blessedness of Giving and Receiving Total Forgiveness.

6. Time

Time is one of man's most precious asset. It is also one access satan always wants to gain into our lives. What you do with your times determines the outcome of your life. We are living at a time when many things are calling for our attention. The Bible says in (Ephesians 5:15-18 [NLT]), *"So be careful how you live. Don't live like fools, but like those who are wise. Make the most of every opportunity in these evil days. Don't act thoughtlessly, but understand what the Lord wants you to do. Don't be drunk with wine, because that will ruin your life. Instead, be filled with the Holy Spirit,"* and (Colossians 4:5 [NLT]), *"Live wisely among those who are not believers, and make the most of every opportunity."*

The King James Version uses the word "Redeeming the time." In both verses, you see Apostle Paul equating the use of time with wisdom. Many people live like there is no tomorrow, they invest their time frivolities that opens the door to satan, yet they wonder why they are attacked. What do you invest your time in? Are you always in church during church services or you see going to church as a waste of time? Do you take time to pray and study the Word or you use the time to post on social media? What are you using your time for?

Gradually the devil is taking over the TV space with programs that can keep you glued with your screen all day. Unfortunately, many people have fallen into his bait. But it's time to audit our time.

Samson is an example of one man who spent his time visiting brothels and women and eventually he met one who lured him into destruction. A strong man who fought against God's enemy as one man was defeated by the same enemy because he had all the time to invest with women rather than God's people. The question again, are you redeeming your time?

Redeem is a word most used when you want to rescue something or someone from captivity. So, God is saying don't allow satan to take your time captive, redeem it. Redeem it daily on the right things. Redeem it daily with the right people. Use your time for God's glory.

Friend, what are you hiding now that seems like no one is seeing you? What area of your life are you lowering the hedge gradually thinking you are still in charge? What space are you giving to the devil to gain grounds in your life? It's time to lock the door and stay focused. The enemy outside the door is not your friend but your enemy. He is not here for fun but for war. So keep fighting and you shall win.

Chapter 8

EXERCISING YOUR SPIRITUAL AUTHORITY

Have you ever been stopped by a young lady or man in police uniform for surpassing the speed limit in an area? Just as you raced through to meet up with your next appointment, you heard the police siren blaring behind you. Then you glanced through the rearview mirror to observe who the siren was escorting and gbam! It's right behind your car. You thought to yourself, I can't remember requesting for police escort, but before your mind rolled to the second thought, you saw the police car light flashing at you and you were pulled over and a young officer like the age of your third child stepped out of the vehicle and requested for your driver's license and vehicle papers. "Sir, you were moving beyond the speed limit and I may have to give you a ticket for that."

Seeing the lady officer in uniform, do you raise your voice and shut her up like you do to your child, or you simply apologizes and accept the necessary punishment? Well, I think at that point the officer age doesn't matter, not even his or her stature or skin color. So long as the officer is well kitted in police uniform, your opinion is not relevant, the officer is in position to put you in order.

This instance brings to our attention the difference between power and authority. Power is said to be the ability of an individual to influence others and control their actions, while authority is the legal and formal right to give orders and commands. Power may be a personal trait whereas authority is a formal right, vested in the hands of a high officials or management personnel. In other words, authority is delegated power. When you are in authority, you aren't acting on your own but by virtue of your position.

Too often, believers have emphasized power and even spend hours and days fasting and praying for power. That sounds good and there is nothing bad about power. But there is a higher level of power, which is authority. The devil may bow to our power, but he has no response when we take the place of authority. This authority is not of ours, but it is given by Christ. Christ's delegated authority is one of the greatest advantages of believers in spiritual warfare. But only few believers know how to exercise and grow their authority in Christ.

Let's read an instance during Jesus' ministry when He demonstrated the efficacy of spiritual authority. The Bible says in (Luke 10:1-9 [NKJV]), *"After these things the Lord appointed seventy others also, and sent them two by two before His face into every city and place where He*

Himself was about to go. Then He said to them, "The harvest truly is great, but the laborers are few; therefore pray the Lord of the harvest to send out laborers into His harvest. Go your way; behold, I send you out as lambs among wolves. Carry neither money bag, knapsack, nor sandals; and greet no one along the road. But whatever house you enter, first say, 'Peace to this house.' And if a son of peace is there, your peace will rest on it; if not, it will return to you. And remain in the same house, eating and drinking such things as they give, for the laborer is worthy of his wages. Do not go from house to house. Whatever city you enter, and they receive you, eat such things as are set before you. And heal the sick there, and say to them, 'The kingdom of God has come near to you.'"

Now, what was the outcome of this assignment? Let's read further in (Luke 10:17-19 [ASV]), *"And the seventy returned with joy, saying, Lord, even the demons are subject unto us in thy name. And he said unto them, I beheld satan fallen as lightning from heaven. Behold, I have given you authority to tread upon serpents and scorpions, and over all the power of the enemy: and nothing shall in any wise hurt you."*

This assignment was one that sent a signal to the kingdom of darkness that some people are coming. Perhaps the powers of darkness only saw Jesus as the threat to contend with. They felt Jesus was one-man army like Samson and so once they kill Him, the battle is won. So, all efforts was on Jesus. The criticism, the insults and even the accusation were all against Jesus until He was crucified. They just watched the disciples walk free. What the kingdom of darkness didn't know is the principle of authority and how relevant it is in God's end time agenda.

Jesus told the disciples, "I didn't just send you out, I sent you with authority." Like that young police officer who carried the full weight of government power, they also carried the full weight of kingdom power. Jesus told them they had authority to mess the kingdom of darkness up with an assurance that they couldn't hurt them. In the US, assaulting a police officer is considered a violent felony. Usually, it attracts a prison term from two years to life imprisonment and a fine. It is true that the court of law takes all forms of assault seriously, however, assault against a police officer is considered horrendous.[16]

Now you understand what Jesus meant when he told His disciples to tread on serpents and whatever the enemy represents and rest assured that they can't be assaulted. They should move with that authority that no devil can assault them. And this truth was demonstrated when they returned. The Bible says they came back excited because although they weren't Jesus, the devils were subject to them in His name. Awesome! Jesus then jumped for joy because what seems like a dress rehearsal worked perfectly. He was excited because now He knew that satan is in trouble. He knows that if He can entrust more saints with this authority, then the kingdom of God will dominate the earth.

This mindset is needed to live a victorious life. The Bible says in (James 4:7 [KJV]), *"Submit yourselves therefore to God. Resist the devil, and he will flee from you."* We have an assurance that satan will flee when we stand in the place of our authority and resist him. Just as a police officer tells an offender, "Put your hands behind your back," and straight away the die-hard thief surrenders, likewise we can command satan to get off our lives based on our authority in Christ.

Who Is The Authority For?

Now, is spiritual authority something you get after twenty years of accepting Christ? Or perhaps you are thinking it's for pastors alone and not for me. Or maybe you need to go to the school of authority like military school to be given this authority. No, it's for everyone that is saved. It is for everyone that believes in Christ. After salvation you have been commissioned to walk in Jesus' spiritual authority against all the forces of darkness.

Jesus said before His departure in (Matthew 28:18-20 [ASV]), *"And Jesus came to them and spake unto them, saying, All authority hath been given unto me in heaven and on earth. Go ye therefore, and make disciples of all the nations, baptizing them into the name of the Father and of the Son and of the Holy Spirit: teaching them to observe all things whatsoever I commanded you: and lo, I am with you always, even unto the end of the world."* He went to the grave to secure the power and authority from satan and He has entrusted it on us. "But He was referring to His disciples not me."

Let's see the account in (Mark 16:15-18 [NIV]), *"He said to them, "Go into all the world and preach the gospel to all creation. Whoever believes and is baptized will be saved, but whoever does not believe will be condemned. And these signs will accompany those who believe: In my name they will drive out demons; they will speak in new tongues; they will pick up snakes with their hands; and when they drink deadly poison, it will not hurt them at all; they will place their hands-on sick people, and they will get well."* Here Jesus used the word, "anyone that believes." Do you believe in Jesus as your Lord and Savior? Then you have that authority also. That power to tread on serpent and cast out demons. You are fortified to walk amidst the activities of darkness without getting hurt. This is awesome.

Apostle Paul said in (1 Corinthians 2:4-5 [ESV]), *"and my speech and my message were not in plausible words of wisdom, but in demonstration of the Spirit and of power, so that your faith might not rest in the wisdom of men but in the power of God."* He wasn't preaching to persuade people with eloquent speeches but he demonstrated the power of Jesus which He received. He knew that the web of darkness over the heart of people only understands power so, there is no need speaking in queens English, because he only bows down to power.

Friend, that concern in your life would only bow to power. You have been given that authority, all you need to do is to exercise it. Authority not exercised is only a power, you need to raise your hand up like a police officer attempting to stop an oncoming vehicle and without hesitation the driver will press the breaks to stop. You need to raise your hand to stop that demonic flow in your life. Raise your hand and exercise the authority you have in Christ not to discuss with serpents but to tread on them. Jesus trained His disciples to spiritual authority and He wants to train you also. He didn't give us words, but authority which empowers our words.

Know Where You Are Positioned

Where are you seated? Where are you positioned in the spirit realm? Now remember the different spiritual hierarchy described in (Ephesians 6:12 [ESV]), *"For we do not wrestle against flesh and blood, but against the rulers, against the authorities, against the cosmic powers over this present darkness, against the spiritual forces of evil in the heavenly places."* These are different levels of spiritual positioning. You will agree with me that in an organization, you can only control people that are below you on the company's organizational chart. You only suggest to those above you and take orders from them. Most believers think they are below all spiritual forces because they live on the earth. My friend, that's not true. You are positioned high above. Not by your fleshly rank but your spiritual authority given to you by Jesus Christ.

The Bible says in (Ephesians 2:1-6 [NLT]), *"Once you were dead because of you and your many sins. You used to live in sin, just like the rest of the world, obeying the devil—the commander of the powers in the unseen world. He is the spirit at work in the hearts of those who refuse* *to obey God. All of us used to live that way, following the passionate desires and inclinations of our sinful nature. By our very nature we were subject to God's anger, just like everyone else. But God is so rich in mercy, and He loved us so much, that even though we were dead because of our sins, He gave us life when He raised Christ from the dead. (It is only by God's grace that we have been saved!) For He raised us from the dead along with Christ and seated us with Him in the heavenly realms because we are united with Christ Jesus. "*I want you to read this portion again.

Before you got saved, the Scripture says you were obeying the devil. Your life was subject to his command and dictates because you were obviously below. But something happened at the cross. The Scripture says you were raised along with Christ. The same power that raised Christ from the dead after three days raised you and elevated you. You are now seated in heavenly places. You are no longer subject to satan's dictates, you are now positioned higher. Just like an employee who gains promotion and now a member of the company's board, such person no longer takes orders, but is now part of the decision making body in that organization. Pause and think about this for a moment.

See how Apostle Paul put it again in (Ephesians 1:18-23 [NIV]), *"I pray also that the eyes of your heart may be enlightened in order that you may know the hope to which he has called you, the riches of his glorious inheritance in the saints, and his incomparably great power for us who believe. That power is like the working of His mighty strength, which He exerted in Christ when He raised Him from the dead and seated Him at His right hand in the heavenly realms, far above all rule and authority, power and dominion, and every title that can be given, not only in the present age but also in the one to come. And God placed all things under His feet and appointed Him to be head over everything for the church, which is His body, the fullness of Him who fills everything in every way."*

This chapter is not trying to give you authority, you have it already, but I want your eyes of understanding to be enlighten to see where you are. It is observed that it takes about 3 days for a spacecraft to travel from the earth to the moon. An average distance of about 240,000 miles (386,400 kilometers).[17] Now imagine how long it takes to reach that beautiful object that show up at night. It looks close but it's far. Now, the Scriptures says you are positioned far above. Meaning, we can't even calculate how far you are positioned from the forces of darkness. Remember that some of these forces are said to be in high places, yet, you are seated with Christ far above them. The Apostle went further to say that they are positioned under your feet for you to tread on them. Hallelujah!

Let this understanding drill into your spirit. Yes, you live in the physical world with families, near the stadium, grocery stores, train station, and movie theatres, but spiritually you are positioned high. God created the physical and spiritual realm, so you need to activate your spiritual authority so you can see the manifestation in the physical realm.

So it's time to open your spiritual eyes to see the happenings around you. You can't win the battle of life when you have your physical eyes fully opened and you shut your spiritual eyes. To walk with authority requires the use of your spiritual eyes to see what is behind the physical activities around you. Through your spiritual eyes, you can pick the driving factors behind the physical realm.

So, you need to ask God to reveal to you what is behind physical situations you are passing through. We are quick to rationalize the events around our lives but when we ask God to reveal to us, we see the real forces responsible for the sickness that won't go away, the failing relationships, the financial breakdown and stagnations. Then we can exercise our authority to stop the negative flow.

When your eyes is open then you can speak with authority and declare boldly what ought not to be. You can resist the devil and he will flee from your life. Don't smile with the enemy, stop crying when you can command him, you have the authority to deal with him, as you speak out loud in Jesus' name.

Friend, don't be carried away with worldly authority without power. People cheat, kill and lie to gain physical authority, yet they are tormented by evil forces. Why? They have no place in the spirit. The spiritual will always control the physical, so seek to gain and exercise your spiritual authority. Strive to maintain your spiritual position by maintaining a quality walk with God. Maintain your stand and you will always see satan fall like lightning before you.

Chapter 9

DISCERNING SATAN'S SUBTLY

Subtlety is one of the enemy's greatest weapons against believers. He loves to cloak his attacks so that we don't know what he's doing. That's why the Bible reveals we wrestle not against flesh and blood. In other words, the enemy isn't coming with obvious look and appearances that can easily be detected.

Another unfortunate truth is the enemy hides behind people and circumstances to ensure that we fight the wrong battles. It's like a doctor treating a patient for cancer when in actual sense, the patient is suffering from bacteria infection. You will agree with me that the patient will not get any better, and while the medical practitioners focus on cancer, the infection keeps spreading until the patient's immune system is completely compromised. This is the reason most believers lose their lives in battle. The devil masks like a friend when in fact he is an enemy.

The Bible says in (Genesis 3:1 [ESV]), *"Now the serpent was more crafty than any other beast of the field that the LORD God had made. He said to the woman, "Did God actually say, 'You shall not eat of any tree in the garden'?"*

Something that is subtle is not immediately obvious or noticeable.[18] Also, a subtle person cleverly uses indirect methods to achieve something.[19] This is the exact nature of the enemy. In the earlier chapters of the book of Genesis, we saw what God created that it was very good: the light, the sea, plants, planets, animals and even human beings. All was good, but the third chapter took a different turn where we see the serpent creeping into the garden.

We understand from the New Testament in Mathew chapter 8 how demons possessed pigs, this implies that demons can possess both human and animals. They always look for a body to manifest on the earth so they can control by taking over their will. This was exemplified when a herd of pig rushed into the water and died. So, perhaps in Genesis chapter 3 when the Bible said serpent came to Eve, it is perfectly possible that an evil spirit took over a snake in the Garden of Eden. In this case this was satan himself. Apostle Paul referred to his subtlety in (2 Corinthians 11:14 [KJV]), *"And no marvel; for satan himself is transformed into an angel of light."* John clearly refers to him in (Revelations 20:2 [KJV]), *"And he laid hold on the dragon, that old serpent, which is the devil, and satan, and bound him a thousand years."*

Perhaps satan appeared as a snake in the Garden because he wanted Eve to think she could handle him.

Remember that God already gave man dominion over all the animals. So you would imagine one of your subordinate trying to play clever. You simply shut him up. So by appearing to Eve as a snake, an animal beneath Eve, satan expect that she would underestimate him.

How often do we also fall for the devils subtle appearance? We simply allow him into our sphere thinking we could control the situation. Alas! We become victims. The devil would have us believe we are in charge until we let our guards down he takes over from there. Even started on a defensive not but then the conversation became friendly until she lost the battle.

It started like a casual conversation about whether the same fruits they see every day until they realized it was a crucial battle that will determine the fate of the entire human race. They were negotiating the future of souls yet unborn thinking it was a mere discussion to compare the importance of one fruit to the other- a certain fruit was safe to eat, a conversation she probably thought she could handle. The outcome was a curse and eviction from the Garden. I pray that you shall not fall prey to the subtlety of satan.

The Bible says in (1 Peter 5:8 [ESV]), *"Be sober-minded; be watchful. Your adversary the devil prowls around like a roaring lion, seeking someone to devour."* To prowl means to move quietly trying not to be seen or heard.[20] He is there but tries to appear otherwise. So when Jesus taught us to pray he asked us to pray that God would deliver us from the evil one. By our strength we can't discern his tricks but with the help of the Spirit of God, we can unmask him and deal decisively with him.

His aim is to destroy our connection with God and leave us vulnerable. He wants to stripe us naked like he did with Adam and Eve, so, stay awake and alert. He is out there consistently masking up like a friend. Wake up and discern what does not represent God. Whatever tries to negotiate your devotion or commitment to God must be stopped. Anything that tried to lower God's standard of holiness and purity should be cut off. It's a battle and not just a casual conversation.

Chapter 10

CONCLUSION

I'm glad you have started this journey with me to this point. I want you to understand that victory is possible. You are not a failure but a victor. Jesus came to deliver us from all the tricks of the devil. He has made provision for our sin and He is ready to help us up. I want you to live from the standpoint of victory from now. Don't give up because you fell. Stand up and keep moving.

Now you see that the battle is on and it is largely spiritual. So, be a person of the Spirit. The Scripture says in (Galatians 5:24-25 [KJV]), *"And they that are Christ's have crucified the flesh with the affections and lusts. If we live in the Spirit, let us also walk in the Spirit."* You are saved in the Spirit, in fact you are a spirit being, so walk in the spirit. Be a man of the spirit. When you do, God will start to open your eyes to see the evil forces around you.

I have been to churches where satan's agents are having a field day. But through the lens of the Spirit, I'm able to see that nothing is natural. So be a person of the

Spirit. Rebuild your walk with God and avoid falling to the trick of complacency. Rather, remain hot for God.

In the next phase of this inspiring book, we shall learn the various spiritual armory to quench all the darts of the wicked one. So, grab a copy of it and arm your spirit man because the battle is still on and you are more than a conqueror.

ENDNOTES

1   Kenneth E. Hagin, *Spiritual Warfare* (2023), publication
    date April 20, 2023, https://sites.google.com/view/spiritu-
    al-warfare-by-kenneth- (accessed June 20, 2023).

2   *Kregel Articles.* "What Is Spiritual Warfare?" https://www.
    kregel.com/articles/what-is-spiritual-warfare-7754(ac-
    cessed June 20, 2023).

3   Campbell, Jac Judy A. "I'm Going There." *Family Friend
    Poems*, August 2016. https://www.familyfriendpoems.
    com/poem/im-going-there.

4   All Round Jesus. "What Is Spiritual Warfare in the Bible?"
    All Round Jesus. https://allroundjesus.com/spiritual-war-
    fare/ (accessed June 20, 2023).

5   *St. Catherine University.* "Title of the Specific Article"
    (if available). https://sophia.stkate.edu/cgi/viewcontent.
    cgi?article=1128&context=msw_papers (accessed June 20,
    2023).

6   Charlotte Elliott, "Christian, seek not yet repose" (1836),
    tune: VIGILATE (Monk), published in 203 hymnals,
    https://hymnary.org/text/christian_seek_not_yet_repose
    (accessed June 20, 2023).

7   Kenneth Copeland Ministries. "4 Strategies the Enemy
    Uses to Keep You Defeated." *Kenneth Copeland Minis-
    tries Blog.* https://blog.kcm.org/4-strategies-enemy-us-
    es-keep-defeated/ (accessed June 20, 2023).

8   AMA (American Management Association). "Know The

Enemy in Order to Win." *AMA.* https://www.amanet.org/articles/to-win-understand-your-enemy/ (accessed June 20, 2023).

9   BrainyQuote. "Jay Shetty - Knowledge is power, and it can help you..." *BrainyQuote.* https://www.brainyquote.com/quotes/jay_shetty_1118675 (accessed June 20, 2023).

10 *Cambridge Dictionary.* "MANIPULATE | English meaning." https://dictionary.cambridge.org/dictionary/english/manipulate (accessed June 20, 2023).

11 *Diana's Diaries.* "3 C's to Win Against the Battle of the Mind." https://dianasdiaries.com/2019/09/15/3-cs-to-win-against-the-battle-of-the-mind/ (accessed June 20, 2023).

12 Hagin, Kenneth E. *The Triumphant Church.* https://christiandiet.com.ng/wp-content/uploads/2019/03/The-Triumphant-Church-Kenneth-E-Hagin.pdf (accessed June 20, 2023).

13 *Bible Study Tools.* "Topos Meaning - Greek Lexicon | New Testament (NAS)." https://www.biblestudytools.com/lexicons/greek/nas/topos.html (accessed June 20, 2023).

14 Mariam. "Show me your friend and I'll tell you who you are." *Goodreads.* https://www.goodreads.com/quotes/592853-show-me-your-friend-and-i-ll-tell-you-who-you (accessed June 20, 2023).

15 *Renner Ministries.* "Don't Give Place to the Devil!" https://renner.org/article/dont-give-place-to-the-devil/ (accessed June 20, 2023).

16 *Meltzer & Bell, P.A.* "Against a Police Officer: What Are the Penalties?" https://www.meltzerandbell.com/news/against-a-police-officer-what-are-the-penalties/ (accessed June 20, 2023).

17 *Cool Cosmos.* "How long does it take to travel to the Moon?" https://coolcosmos.ipac.caltech.edu/ask/174-How-long-does-it-take-to-travel-to-the-Moon-#:~:text=It%20takes%20about%203%20days,on%20the%20specific%20path%20chosen (accessed June 20, 2023).

18 *Collins English Dictionary.* "Subtle definition and meaning." https://www.collinsdictionary.com/us/dictionary/english/subtle#:~:text=in%20British%20English-,(%C-

B%88s%CA%8Ct%C9%99l%20),not%20immediately%20
obvious%20or%20comprehensible (accessed June 20,
2023).

19   *Collins English Dictionary.* "Subtle definition and mean-
     ing." https://www.collinsdictionary.com/us/dictionary/
     english/subtle#:~:text=in%20British%20English-,(%C-
     B%88s%CA%8Ct%C9%99l%20),not%20immediately%20
     obvious%20or%20comprehensible (accessed June 20,
     2023).

20   *Cambridge Dictionary.* "PROWL | English meaning."
     https://dictionary.cambridge.org/dictionary/english/prowl
     (accessed June 20, 2023).